This book belongs to

Age

Favourite player

Prediction of Ipswich Town's final position this season

Prediction of Sky Bet Championship winners this season

Prediction of FA Cup winners this season

Prediction of Capital One Cup winners this season

Prediction of teams to be relegated from the Sky Bet Championship this season:

22nd

23rd

24th

Written by

Contribu
Lee Hyde,
Steve Pearce & Rob Mas

A TWOCAN PUBLICATION

Every effort has been made to ensure the accuracy of information within this publication but the publishers can not be held responsible for any errors or omissions.

Views expressed are those of the author and do not necessarily represent those of the publishers or the football club.

ISBN 978-1-909872-23-3

PICTURE CREDITS

Action Images,
Press Association,
Dan Sakal & Warren Page

£7.99

IPSWICH TOWN
FOOTBALL CLUB

marcus
Evans

IPSWICH TOWN
FOOTBALL CLUB

CONTENTS

If you go to every Tractor Boys game home and away you'll see the players in action for 90 minutes every weekend and sometimes in midweek too. That isn't all the players do though.

WORK HARD PLAY HARDER

Footballers have to spend a lot of time preparing for matches and afterwards assessing how well they have done with the coaching staff. Video-analysts have an important role to play. Every player has his performance examined in detail so the player and coaches can build on his strengths and work on developing areas of weakness. This isn't just for first-team players but young players too.

Much of the hard work to get players fit comes in pre-season when the squad are likely to do a lot of running and working with weights so that players build up the core strength and stamina they'll need to get them through 46 tough championship games, cup ties and possibly Play-Offs at the end of a long gruelling season.

As any player will tell you though, you only get real tip-top match fitness by playing in games. This is why footballers usually only believe they are getting up to their best standard when they have been able to play a few games in a row.

Coaching staff carefully monitor the fitness levels of every player and can give an individual extra work if he needs it. Sometimes coaching staff have to tell a player to rest if he is doing too much because rest and recuperation can be as vital for muscles as time spent in the gym.

It's about getting the balance right so the more games there are to play the less time will be spent on fitness work. Training sessions work on skills, tactics and set-piece routines as well with more and more game focus in the days leading up to a fixture.

IPSWICH TOWN
FOOTBALL CLUB

BLUESNATIONS HUNGARY

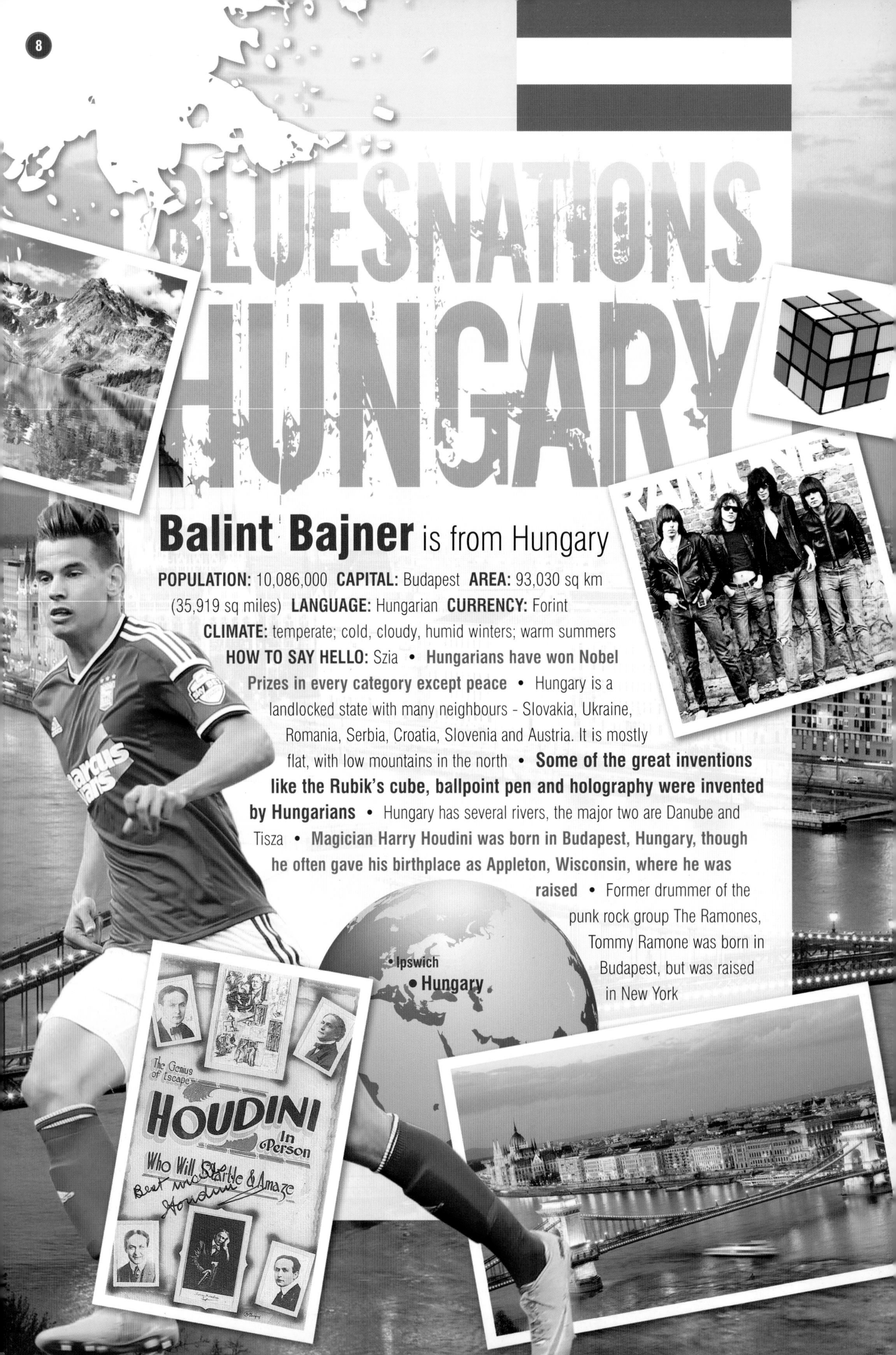

Balint Bajner is from Hungary

POPULATION: 10,086,000 **CAPITAL:** Budapest **AREA:** 93,030 sq km (35,919 sq miles) **LANGUAGE:** Hungarian **CURRENCY:** Forint **CLIMATE:** temperate; cold, cloudy, humid winters; warm summers **HOW TO SAY HELLO:** Szia • **Hungarians have won Nobel Prizes in every category except peace** • Hungary is a landlocked state with many neighbours - Slovakia, Ukraine, Romania, Serbia, Croatia, Slovenia and Austria. It is mostly flat, with low mountains in the north • **Some of the great inventions like the Rubik's cube, ballpoint pen and holography were invented by Hungarians** • Hungary has several rivers, the major two are Danube and Tisza • **Magician Harry Houdini was born in Budapest, Hungary, though he often gave his birthplace as Appleton, Wisconsin, where he was raised** • Former drummer of the punk rock group The Ramones, Tommy Ramone was born in Budapest, but was raised in New York

THE BIG MATCH

Can you match each of these players to the number of goals they scored for Ipswich Town?

JAY EMMANUEL-THOMAS · MICK MILLS · PAUL MARINER · ALAN BRAZIL · RAY CRAWFORD · JASON DOZZELL · ARNOLD MUHREN · MICHAEL CHOPRA · ERIC GATES

54 · 73 · 18 · 204 · 22 · 96 · 70 · 8 · 21

ANSWERS ON PAGE 62

Dean GERKEN

Goalkeeper

01

Nationality: English
DOB: 22.03.1985

A fierce shot-stopper, Gerken managed to dislodge Scott Loach between the sticks last term, as he became Mick McCarthy's first choice goalkeeper throughout his debut season.

Jonathan PARR

Defender

02

Nationality: Norwegian
DOB: 21.10.1988

A solid defender who operates predominately as a left-back but can play in a number of positions. Parr became Mick McCarthy's fourth capture of the summer, after arriving on a free transfer.

Tyrone MINGS

Defender

03

Nationality: English
DOB: 13.03.1993

Mings is a naturally athletic left-back and caught Mick McCarthy's attention after performing well for Chippenham Town, where he played alongside Town's former U18 coach Russell Osman's son, Toby.

THE SQUAD

Tommy SMITH

Defender

05

Nationality: New Zealander
DOB: 31.03.1990

Smith progressed through the Academy ranks at the Club and is now performing for the first-team at the heart of defence. He has also performed well internationally and has represented New Zealand over 25 times.

Luke CHAMBERS

Defender

04

Nationality: English
DOB: 28.09.1985

A central defender, Chambers joined Town in July 2012 on a free transfer and signed a three-year deal. He impressed in his debut season and has since become a regular at the back.

Christophe BERRA

Defender

06

Nationality: Scottish
DOB: 31.01.1985

A towering defender, Berra chose to establish himself on the international scene with Scotland although he was also eligible to play for France through his father. He has represented them over 25 times.

Cameron STEWART

Midfielder

07

Nationality: English
DOB: 08.04.1991

Cameron has good experience of the Championship and Town swooped to seal a deal ahead of the pre-season trip to Ireland. He signed for Ipswich this summer on a free transfer after leaving Hull City.

Daryl MURPHY

Striker

09

Nationality: Irish
DOB: 15.03.1983

A regular since he joined the Club, Murphy brings a wealth of experience to the front line. He is a powerful forward who is also capable of playing on the left-hand side.

Cole SKUSE

Midfielder

08

Nationality: English
DOB: 29.03.1986

Skuse signed a three-year deal with Ipswich Town in May 2013. Although naturally a central midfielder, he can also fill in at right-back and adds experience and steel to the Town ranks.

David McGOLDRICK

Striker

10

Nationality: English
DOB: 29.11.1987

McGoldrick formed a strong partnership with Murphy last season netting 18 goals in 22 games in the first half of the season. A knee injury forced McGoldrick out for the majority of the second half of the season.

Paul ANDERSON

Midfielder

11

Nationality: English
DOB: 23.07.1988

Anderson plays primarily as a winger and can operate on either flank. He signed a two-year deal last summer and featured regularly in the first-team squad during his debut season.

Stephen HUNT

Midfielder

12

Nationality: Irish
DOB: 01.08.1981

Hunt became known for his creative and skilful play as well as his work rate as a winger. He signed a further one-year deal with Town this summer and has also represented Republic of Ireland.

Balint BAJNER

Striker

14

Nationality: Hungarian
DOB: 19.11.1990

A powerful striker, Bajner penned a one -year deal with the option of a further 12 months this summer. He endeared himself to the fans with a stunning goal against Southend in pre-season.

Kevin BRU

Midfielder

17

Nationality: Mauritian
DOB: 12.12.1988

Bru joined Town on a free transfer after leaving Bulgarian side, Levski Sofia. He has played in France, Italy and Bulgaria and has been capped by Mauritius at international level.

IPSWICH TOWN
FOOTBALL CLUB

Jay TABB

Midfielder

18

Nationality: Irish
DOB: 21.02.1984

A talented midfielder, Tabb joined Ipswich Town on a permanent basis last summer. He made his debut against his former club Reading on 3 August 2013 and scored the opener in a 2-1 defeat.

Luke HYAM

Midfielder

19

Nationality: English
DOB: 24.10.1991

Ipswich-born midfielder, Hyam came through the Academy at Portman Road. He brings energy and tenacity to the side and has earned his place as a regular in the first-team.

Frederic **Veseli**

Defender

20

Nationality: Swiss
DOB: 20.11.1992

Veseli joined Ipswich Town in July 2013 on a two-year deal. He has represented Switzerland at every level of youth football, and captained the Switzerland U17s to victory in the 2009 FIFA U17 World Cup.

Anthony **WORDSWORTH**

Midfielder

22

Nationality: English
DOB: 03.01.1989

A cultured midfielder who signed for Town last January. Wordsworth had spent only three days training with Blues before he'd done enough to convince Mick McCarthy that he was worthy of a permanent stay.

Elliott **HEWITT**

Defender

21

Nationality: Welsh
DOB: 30.05.1994

A young full-back, Elliott was attracting the interest of a number of Premier League and Championship clubs before signing a three-year deal in May 2012 and has impressed in his performances in a Blue shirt so far.

IPSWICH TOWN
FOOTBALL CLUB

Alex HENSHALL

Midfielder

23

Nationality: English
DOB: 15.02.1994

Henshall completed a permanent move to Town this summer and will hope to force his way into Mick McCarthy's plans this season after being named on the bench numerous times while on loan last term.

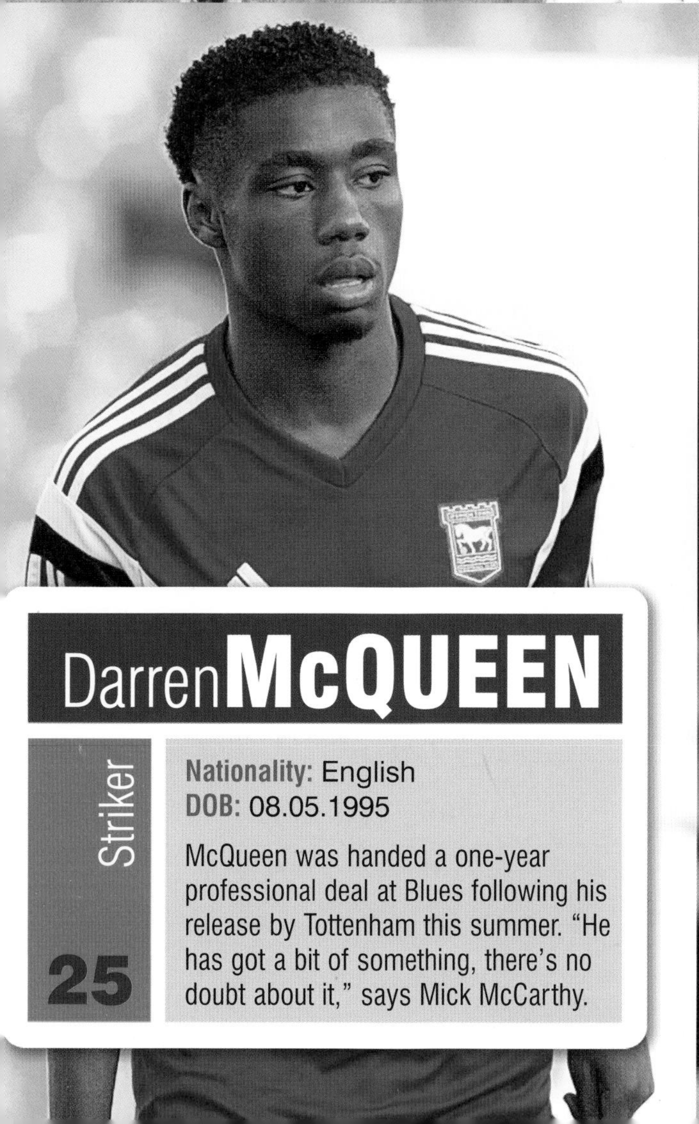

Darren McQUEEN

Striker

25

Nationality: English
DOB: 08.05.1995

McQueen was handed a one-year professional deal at Blues following his release by Tottenham this summer. "He has got a bit of something, there's no doubt about it," says Mick McCarthy.

Paul TAYLOR

Striker

26

Nationality: English
DOB: 04.11.1987

A creative forward player, Paul Taylor possesses enthusiasm and skill in abundance. He is equally at home on either flank or through the middle and has dogged determination, quick feet and flexibility.

Teddy **BISHOP**

Midfielder

27

Nationality: English
DOB: 15.07.1996

Bishop started his career as part of the Ipswich Town academy since the U8s. He made his first-team debut this August in the first round of the League Cup against Crawley Town.

Matt **CLARKE**

Defender

28

Nationality: English
DOB: 22.09.1996

An academy scholar, Clarke is comfortable playing as a midfielder, as well as in his more natural position as a defender. He is highly thought of in the Town academy and has been handed the number 28 shirt for this season.

Ben **WYATT**

Defender

30

Nationality: English
DOB: 04.02.1996

A young left-back, Wyatt joined Ipswich Town from East-Anglian neighbours, Norwich City.
He will be part of the U21 development squad this term.

Conor **SAMMON**

Striker

32

Nationality: Irish
DOB: 06.11.1986

Republic of Ireland international, Sammon joined Ipswich Town on a season-long loan from Derby County on 15 August 2014. He will provide another dimension to Mick McCarthy's frontline.

Bartosz Bialkowski

Goalkeeper

33

Nationality: Polish
DOB: 06.07.1987

A towering shot-stopper, who began his career at Southampton, working alongside current Town 'keeper-coach Malcolm Webster. Bialkowski will compete with Gerken for the number one spot this term.

Frank NOUBLE

Striker

35

Nationality: English
DOB: 24.09.1991

A powerful striker, Nouble joined Blues in January 2013 from Championship rivals Wolves, penning an 18 month contract at Portman Road. He has been capped for England at U17 and U19 levels.

Jack MARRIOTT

Striker

34

Nationality: English
DOB: 09.09.1994

A young forward, Marriott has progressed through the Academy ranks at Portman Road. A regular for the U18s and U21 Development side, he will be hoping to push on into the first-team this term.

THE GOOD OLD DAYS 1960s

	Division	Position
1959-60	Division 2	11th of 22
1960-61	Division 2	1st of 22
1961-62	Division 1	1st of 22
1962-63	Division 1	17th of 22
1963-64	Division 1	22nd of 22
1964-65	Division 2	5th of 22
1965-66	Division 2	15th of 22
1966-67	Division 2	5th of 22
1967-68	Division 2	1st of 22
1968-69	Division 1	12th of 22

Ipswich Town manager Alf Ramsey talks to his new signings about the challenge they will face in the coming months: (l-r) Roy Stephenson, Ray Crawford, Doug Moran and Jimmy Leadbetter

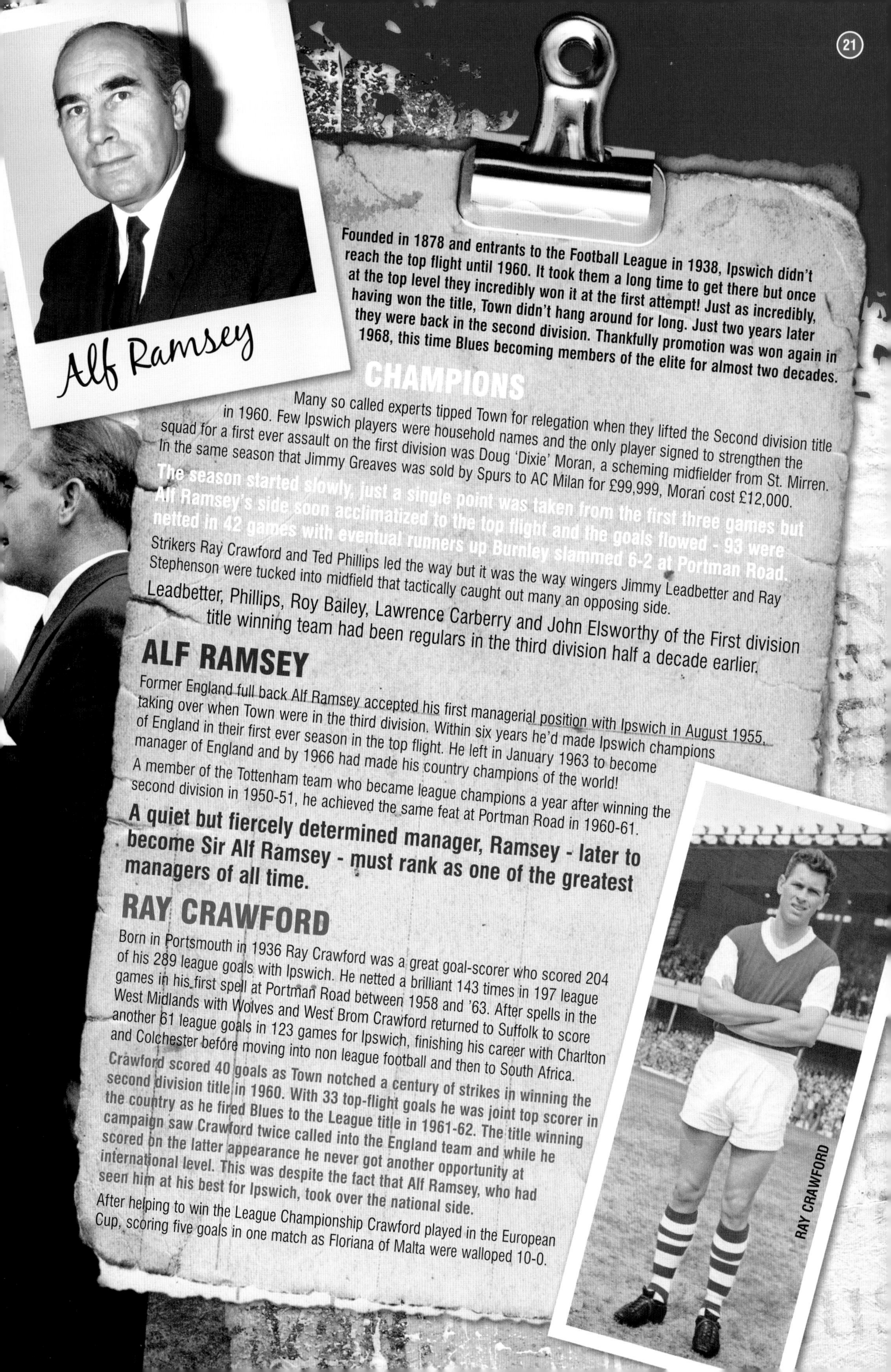

Founded in 1878 and entrants to the Football League in 1938, Ipswich didn't reach the top flight until 1960. It took them a long time to get there but once at the top level they incredibly won it at the first attempt! Just as incredibly, having won the title, Town didn't hang around for long. Just two years later they were back in the second division. Thankfully promotion was won again in 1968, this time Blues becoming members of the elite for almost two decades.

CHAMPIONS

Many so called experts tipped Town for relegation when they lifted the Second division title in 1960. Few Ipswich players were household names and the only player signed to strengthen the squad for a first ever assault on the first division was Doug 'Dixie' Moran, a scheming midfielder from St. Mirren. In the same season that Jimmy Greaves was sold by Spurs to AC Milan for £99,999, Moran cost £12,000.

The season started slowly, just a single point was taken from the first three games but Alf Ramsey's side soon acclimatized to the top flight and the goals flowed - 93 were netted in 42 games with eventual runners up Burnley slammed 6-2 at Portman Road.

Strikers Ray Crawford and Ted Phillips led the way but it was the way wingers Jimmy Leadbetter and Ray Stephenson were tucked into midfield that tactically caught out many an opposing side.

Leadbetter, Phillips, Roy Bailey, Lawrence Carberry and John Elsworthy of the First division title winning team had been regulars in the third division half a decade earlier.

ALF RAMSEY

Former England full back Alf Ramsey accepted his first managerial position with Ipswich in August 1955, taking over when Town were in the third division. Within six years he'd made Ipswich champions of England in their first ever season in the top flight. He left in January 1963 to become manager of England and by 1966 had made his country champions of the world!

A member of the Tottenham team who became league champions a year after winning the second division in 1950-51, he achieved the same feat at Portman Road in 1960-61.

A quiet but fiercely determined manager, Ramsey - later to become Sir Alf Ramsey - must rank as one of the greatest managers of all time.

RAY CRAWFORD

Born in Portsmouth in 1936 Ray Crawford was a great goal-scorer who scored 204 of his 289 league goals with Ipswich. He netted a brilliant 143 times in 197 league games in his first spell at Portman Road between 1958 and '63. After spells in the West Midlands with Wolves and West Brom Crawford returned to Suffolk to score another 61 league goals in 123 games for Ipswich, finishing his career with Charlton and Colchester before moving into non league football and then to South Africa.

Crawford scored 40 goals as Town notched a century of strikes in winning the second division title in 1960. With 33 top-flight goals he was joint top scorer in the country as he fired Blues to the League title in 1961-62. The title winning campaign saw Crawford twice called into the England team and while he scored on the latter appearance he never got another opportunity at international level. This was despite the fact that Alf Ramsey, who had seen him at his best for Ipswich, took over the national side.

After helping to win the League Championship Crawford played in the European Cup, scoring five goals in one match as Floriana of Malta were walloped 10-0.

IPSWICH TOWN FOOTBALL CLUB

THE TEAM

2014-15

BIRMINGHAM CITY

GROUND: St Andrew's **CAPACITY:** 30,016
MANAGER: Lee Clark **NICKNAME:** Blues

DID YOU KNOW: Founded as Small Heath, they played in the Football Alliance before becoming founder members and first ever champions of the Football League Second Division.

BLACKBURN ROVERS

GROUND: Ewood Park **CAPACITY:** 31,367
MANAGER: Gary Bowyer
NICKNAMES: Rovers, Blue and Whites

DID YOU KNOW: Blackburn Rovers' Latin motto is 'Arte et labore', the club's translation of which is 'By Skill and Hard Work'.

BLACKPOOL

GROUND: Bloomfield Road
CAPACITY: 17,338 **MANAGER:** José Riga
NICKNAMES: The Seasiders, The 'Pool, The Tangerines

DID YOU KNOW: Blackpool won the FA Cup in 1953.

BOLTON WANDERERS

GROUND: Macron Stadium **CAPACITY:** 28,723
MANAGER: Dougie Freedman
NICKNAMES: The Trotters, The Whites, The White Men, The Men in White

DID YOU KNOW: Bolton have won the FA Cup four times - in 1923, 1926, 1929 and 1958.

MEET YOUR RIVALS

Time to get to grips with the teams the Tractor Boys will be facing this season...

AFC BOURNEMOUTH

GROUND: Goldsands Stadium **CAPACITY:** 10,783
MANAGER: Eddie Howe **NICKNAME:** The Cherries

DID YOU KNOW: They won promotion to the Championship at the end of the 2012/13, putting them in the second tier of the league for only the 2nd time in their history.

BRENTFORD

GROUND: Griffin Park **CAPACITY:** 12,300
MANAGER: Mark Warburton
NICKNAME: The Bees

DID YOU KNOW: Brentford's most successful spell came during the 1930s, when they achieved consecutive top six finishes in the First Division.

BRIGHTON & HOVE ALBION

GROUND: The AMEX Stadium
CAPACITY: 30,750 **HEAD COACH:** Sami Hyypiä
NICKNAMES: The Seagulls, The Albion

DID YOU KNOW: Brighton has a number of celebrity fans, including commentator, Des Lynam, DJ, Fat Boy Slim and comic genius, Norman Wisdom.

CARDIFF CITY

GROUND: Cardiff City Stadium
CAPACITY: 28,018 **MANAGER:** Ole Gunnar Solskjær **NICKNAME:** The Bluebirds

DID YOU KNOW: Cardiff City is the only club from outside England to have won the FA Cup, which they won in 1927.

CHARLTON ATHLETIC

GROUND: The Valley **CAPACITY:** 27,111
HEAD COACH: Bob Peeters
NICKNAME: The Addicks

DID YOU KNOW: Charlton were rare among football clubs, they reserved a seat on their directors' board for a supporter! (until 2008, when legal issues stopped them)

DERBY COUNTY

GROUND: iPro Stadium **CAPACITY:** 33,597
MANAGER: Steve McClaren
NICKNAME: The Rams

DID YOU KNOW: Derby County are one of only ten clubs to have competed in every season of the English football league!

FULHAM

GROUND: Craven Cottage **CAPACITY:** 25,700
MANAGER (CARETAKER): Kit Symons
NICKNAMES: The Whites, The Lilywhites

DID YOU KNOW: Fulham has produced many English greats including Johnny Haynes, George Cohen, Bobby Robson, Rodney Marsh & Alan Mullery.

THE BIG MATCH

Can you match each of these crests to the Championship Club they belong to?

WIGAN ATHLETIC · DERBY COUNTY · BRIGHTON & HOVE ALBION · LEICESTER CITY · NORWICH CITY · FULHAM · WEST BROMWICH ALBION · BURNLEY · CHARLTON ATHLETIC

ANSWERS ON PAGE 62

adidas
marcus evans
9
DARYL
MURPHY
09

PAUL ANDERSON

FOOTIE FIRSTS

What were the first pair of boots you owned? Puma King

Who was the first big influence on your career and why?
My Dad. He helped me with getting into football and always supported me

Who was the first manager you played for - what was he like?
Roberto Martinez, he gave me my first pro game - such a nice guy and a great manager!

BEST...

Best advice you've been given?
Always work hard and keep a good attitude

Best sportsperson in the world? David Beckham

Best moment of my life?
Being born! - Otherwise I wouldn't have any moments

IF I COULD...

Re-live one moment in my career, it would be...?
Representing my country, albeit only at U14 level

Travel back in time, I would...?
Go back to when the world started to see what happened

Be best friends with anyone in the world, it would be...?
I wouldn't change my group of mates

FINALLY...

Something interesting you might not know about me is...?
I'm Beautiful South's number 1 fan as I'm a perfect 10!

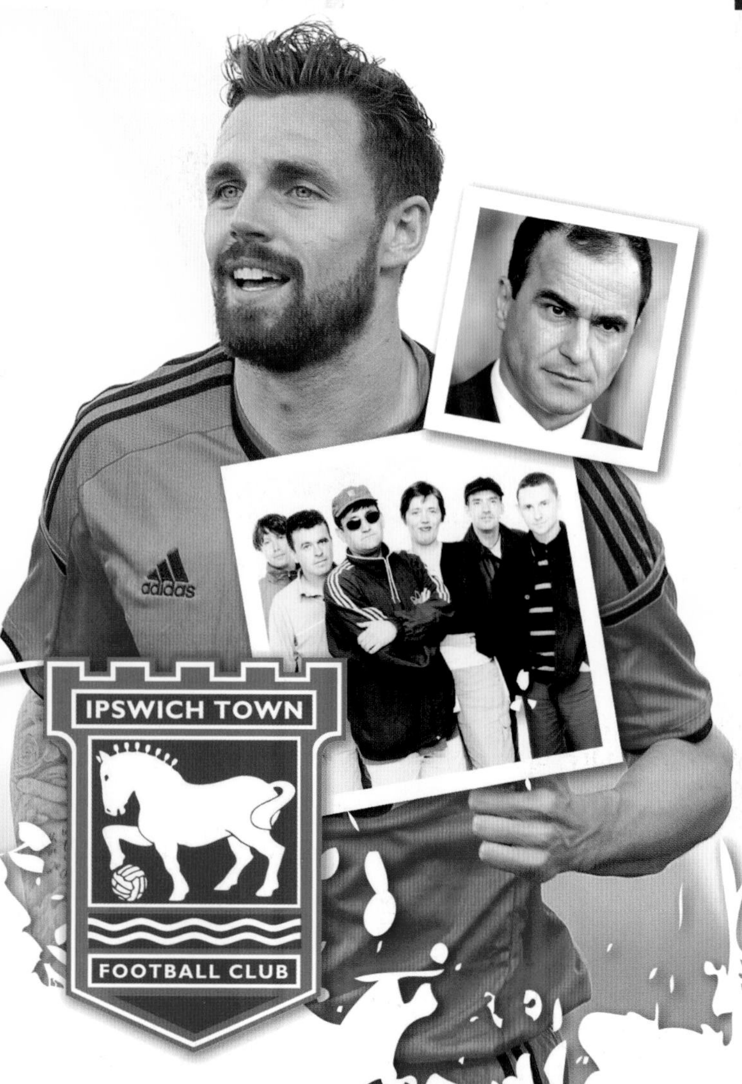

JAY TABB

FOOTIE FIRSTS

What were the first pair of boots you owned? Ryan Giggs' Reeboks

Who was the first manager you played for - what was he like?
A guy called Mike for my Little League team - He was a young wizard and nice guy

Which is your first goal that comes to mind?
My first professional goal for Brentford, away at Barnet

BEST...

Best team you've played against? Man City

Best sportsperson in the world? Roger Federer - Class!

Best moment of my life? On holiday with my brothers

IF I COULD...

Have one superpower, it would be...?
To read people's minds

Travel back in time, I would...?
Go back and experience the sixties

Be best friends with anyone in the world, it would be...?
Prince Harry, I think he'd be a laugh!

FINALLY...

Something interesting you might not know about me is...?
I once started to learn to play the piano and can still play a little bit

CAMERON STEWART

FOOTIE FIRSTS

Who was the first big influence on your career and why?
My Dad, he always took me to training and the park

Who was the first manager you played for - what was he like?
Neil Brown, my Sunday League manager - he loved football!

When were you first spotted by a pro club?
When I was 12 years old playing for my school

BEST...

Best advice you've been given?
Enjoy it but always work hard and your talent will shine through

Best friend in football? Daniel Welbeck and Kyle Bartley - we grew up in the same Sunday League team

Best sportsperson in the world? Roger Federer

IF I COULD...

Play any sportsman at their own game, it would be...?
Michael Jordan at basketball

Travel back in time, I would...?
Go see some dinosaurs

Be best friends with anyone in the world, it would be...?
David Beckham

FINALLY...

Something interesting you might not know about me is...?
I could have been a professional rugby player

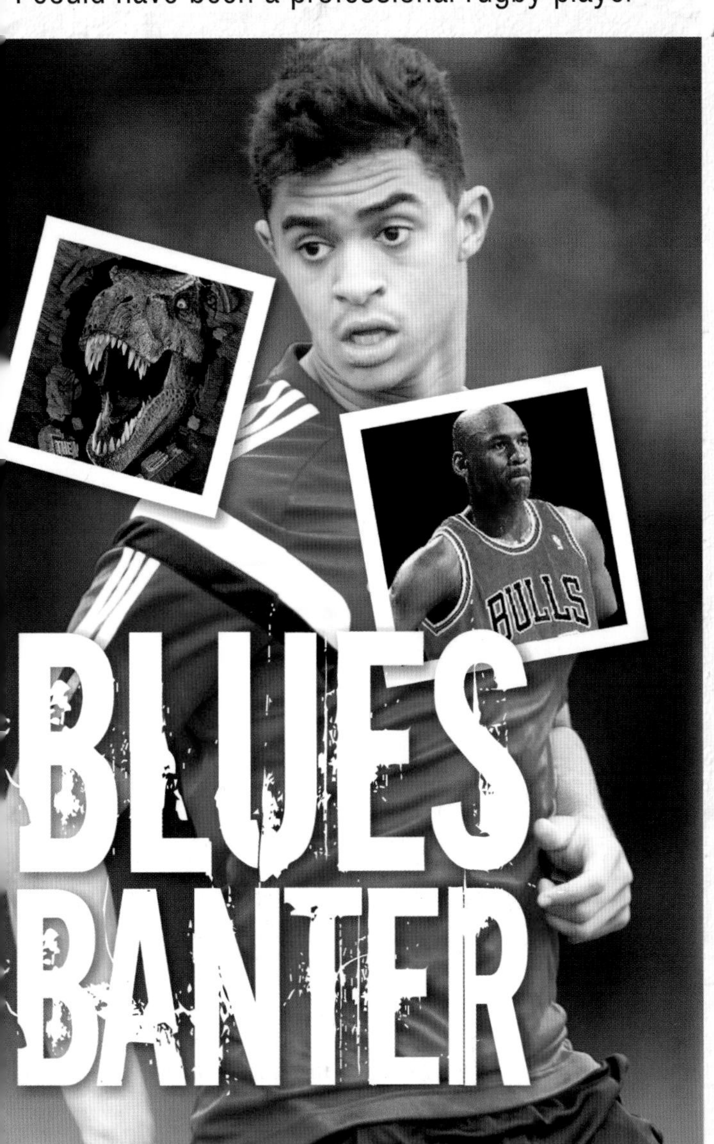

ALEX HENSHALL

FOOTIE FIRSTS

Who was the first big influence on your career and why?
My Dad - we are a big footballing family

Who was the first manager you played for - what was he like?
Clive Page, he was a tactical manager and positive

When were you first spotted by a pro club?
When playing for Ferndale when I was about 11

BEST...

Best advice you've been given?
Always keep your feet on the ground

Best team you've played against? Barcelona

Best moment of my life? Getting into the first team squad at Swindon when I was 15 years old

IF I COULD...

Play any sportsman at their own game, it would be...?
Andy Murray at tennis

Have one superpower, it would be...? Invisibility

Be best friends with anyone in the world, it would be...? David Beckham

FINALLY...

Something interesting you might not know about me is...?
I could have been a tennis pro!

PLAYER OF THE YEAR 2013•14

Striker David McGoldrick was named as Ipswich Town's 'Player of the year', after a stunning first full season at Portman Road. After joining on a free transfer from Nottingham Forest, the forward went on to notch 16 goals and finish as the Blues' top scorer - despite his season being cut short through injury that he suffered against Blackpool in February.

He formed a strong partnership with Daryl Murphy and played in the 'number 10' role for Mick McCarthy's side, coming deep to pick up the ball and start attacking moves for his teammates. Strong on either foot, 'Didz' has also shown a key eye for a spectacular goal such as the brace he scored against Brighton last season.

Much loved by the supporters, the striker has his own song sung to him by the Blue Army to the tune of Seven Nation Army by the White Stripes- 'Oh David McGoldrick'!

David has done well to overcome a knee ligament injury and made his return to action in pre-season, before coming off the bench to score the winner as Town beat Fulham 2-1 on the opening day of this season at Portman Road.

His talents haven't gone unnoticed, however, as Blues fielded several calls for his services on deadline day from the likes of Premier League duo Leicester City and Crystal Palace, but owner Marcus Evans rebuffed the bids and David remains a Town player, to the delight of his manager, teammates and the fans!

He wears the number 10 shirt for Town and his previous clubs include Notts County, Southampton and Nottingham Forest. A little fact you may not know, David actually played against Town for Southampton in the FA Youth Cup final in 2005, which Blues went on to win 3-2.

GOAL OF THE SEASON 2013•14

JONNY WILLIAMS V DERBY COUNTY

Jonny Williams, or 'Joniesta' as he is known by, rocked Portman Road with a stunning strike against Derby County that saw him claim Town's 'goal of the season' award for 2013/14.

The Welsh international, who joined Town on loan from Crystal Palace, really caught the eye with his performances in the middle of the park and quickly emerged as a fan favourite.

And scoring goals like the one he did against Derby are certainly going to help! Town's number 25 picked up the ball around 35 yards from goal, he took one touch before rifling an effort that arrowed behind the palms of Rams 'keeper Lee Grant and flew into the far corner. Portman Road erupted and Town went on to win the game 2-1, thanks to a late winner from Christophe Berra.

It was the only goal Jonny scored for the Blues during his loan spell, but what a goal to score!

GUESS

ANSWERS ON PAGE 62

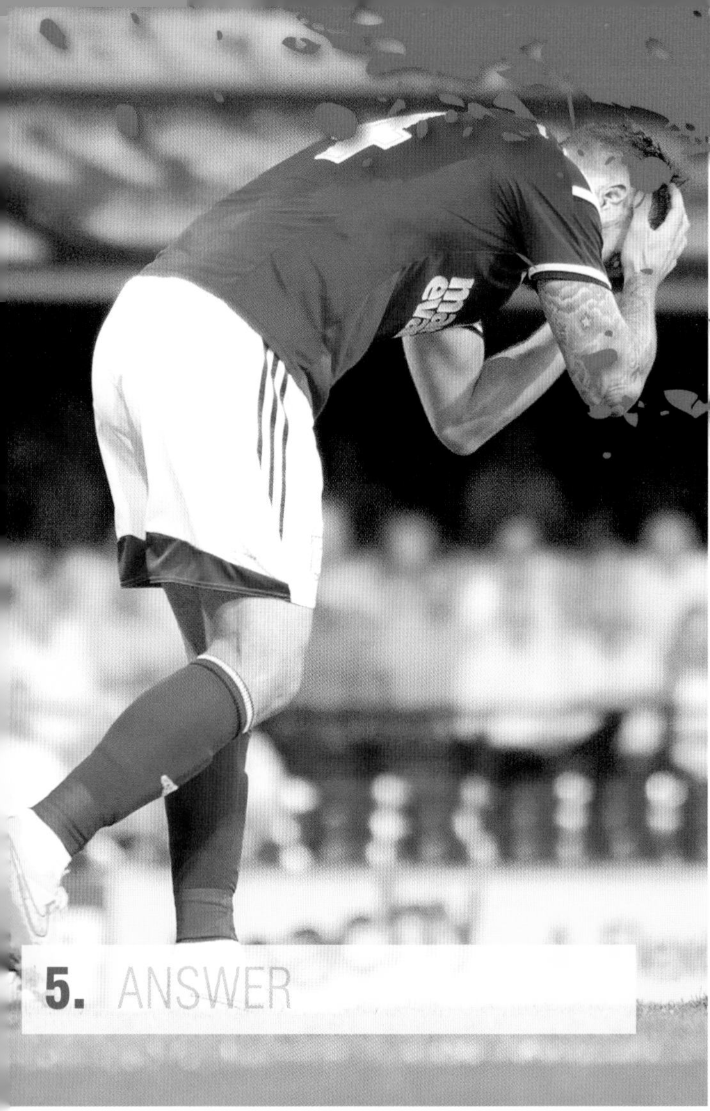

5. ANSWER

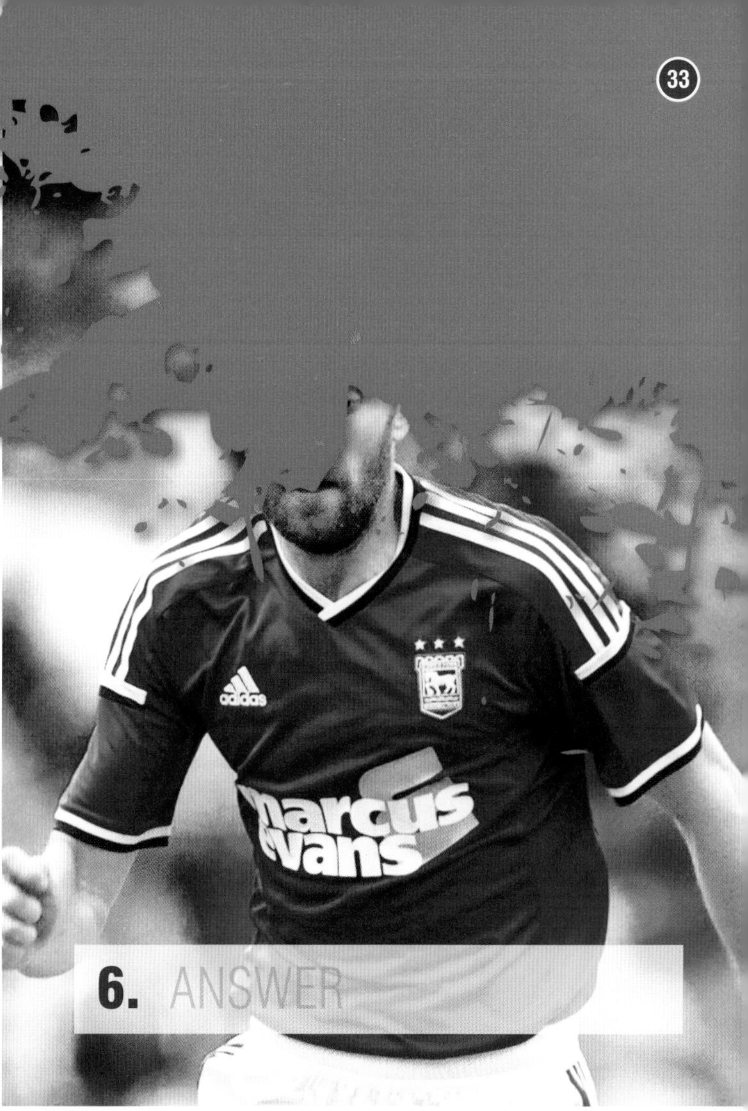

6. ANSWER

WHO

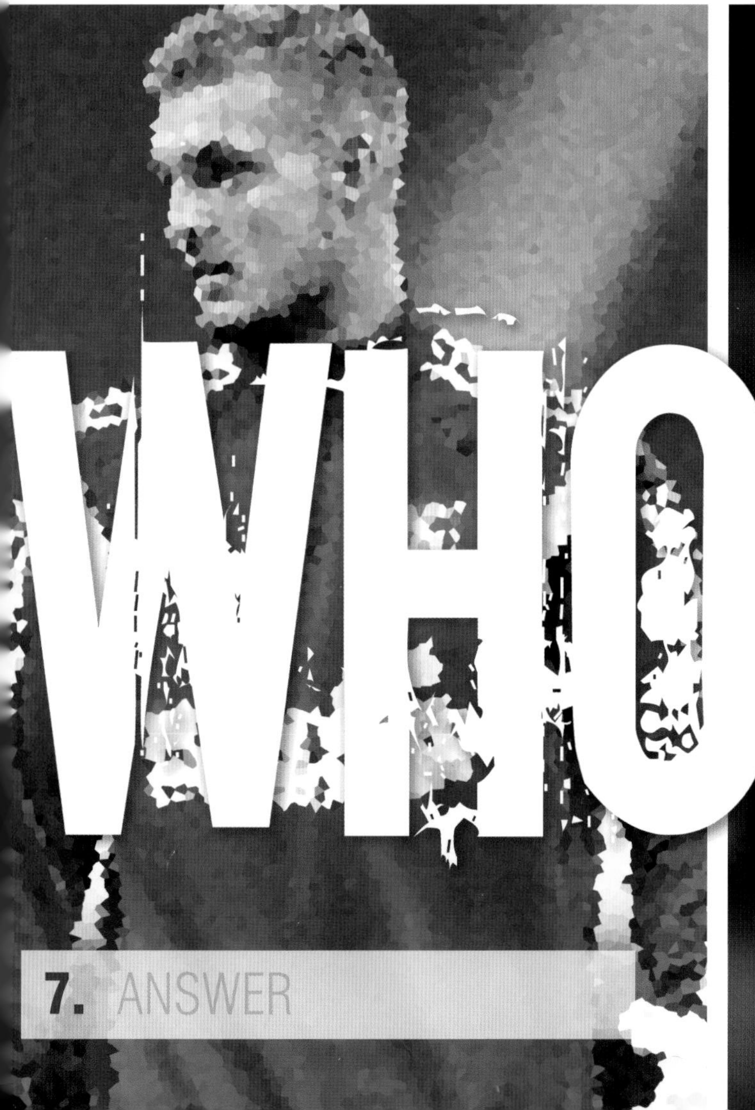

7. ANSWER

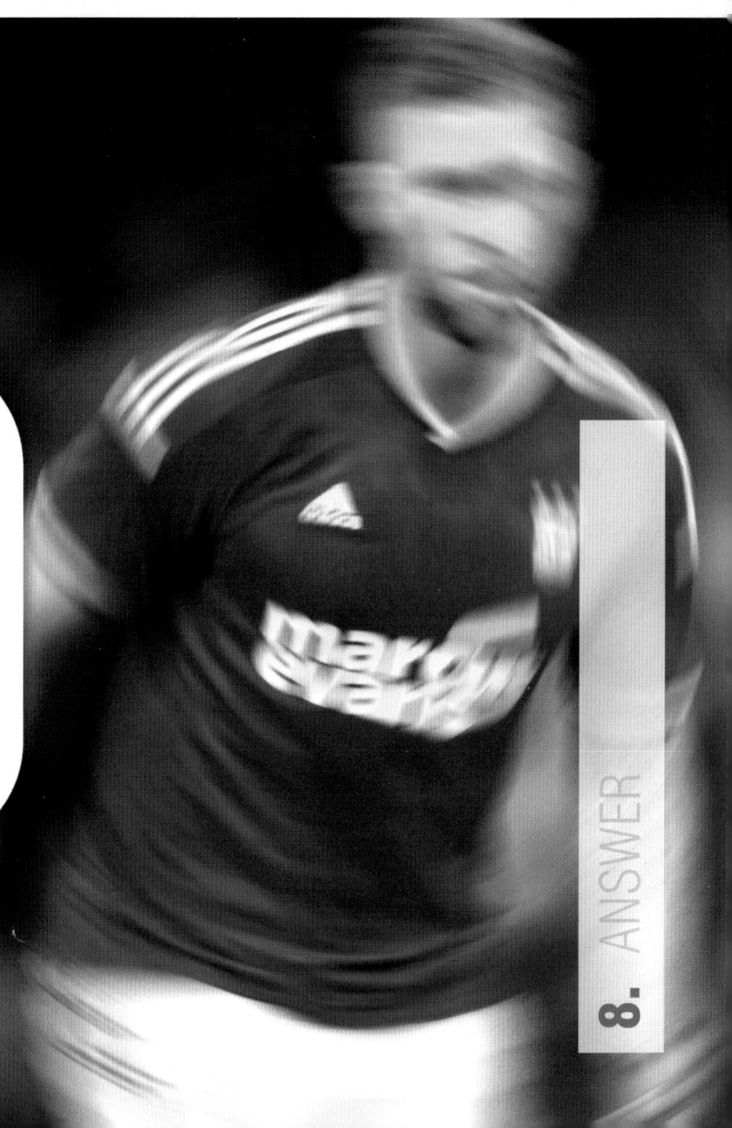

8. ANSWER

LUKE CHAMBERS 04

THE BIG MATCH

Can you match each of these players to the number of league appearances they made for Ipswich Town?

ROGER OSBORNE · CARLOS EDWARDS · TERRY BUTCHER · KEVIN BEATTIE · ALAN HUNTER · MATT HOLLAND · FRANS THIJSSEN · JOHN WARK · GEORGE BURLEY

271 · 228 · 124 · 166 · 258 · 394 · 509 · 125 · 280

A. PLAYER: APPS:

B. PLAYER: APPS:

C. PLAYER: APPS:

D. PLAYER: APPS:

E. PLAYER: APPS:

F. PLAYER: APPS:

G. PLAYER: APPS:

H. PLAYER: APPS:

I. PLAYER: APPS:

ANSWERS ON PAGE 62

THE GOOD OLD DAYS 1970s

SUPER SEVENTIES

The 1970s saw Ipswich play at the top level for the full decade. The most successful season however went hand in hand with the second lowest league placing in the 70s as the FA Cup was sensationally won in 1978. There were also good cup runs in 1974-75 and 1978-79, the FA Youth Cup was twice won and the short-lived Texaco Cup was lifted while European football also returned to Portman Road.

	Division	Position	
1969-70	Division 2	18th of 22	
1970-71	Division 1	19th of 22	
1971-72	Division 1	13th of 22	
1972-73	Division 1	4th of 22	Texaco Cup winners FA Youth Cup winners
1973-74	Division 1	4th of 22	
1974-75	Division 1	3rd of 22	FA Cup semi finalists, League Cup quarter finalists, FA Youth Cup winners
1975-76	Division 1	6th of 22	
1976-77	Division 1	3rd of 22	
1977-78	Division 1	18th of 22	FA Cup winners
1978-79	Division 1	6th of 22	FA Cup quarter finalists

ROGER OSBORNE SCORES, 1978 FA CUP FINAL

John Wark

FA CUP WINNERS

A 76th minute goal from Roger Osborne brought the cup to Suffolk in 1978 and made Osborne a hero.

The cup run had begun with comfortable wins away to Cardiff and at home to Hartlepool before a replay was needed to overcome Bristol Rovers and move into the quarter-finals. A hat-trick from Paul Mariner helped Town to sweep Millwall aside with a handsome 6-1 victory.

Arsenal's Highbury stadium was the venue for the semi-final meeting with West Bromwich Albion where Brian Talbot, Mick Mills and midfield marksman John Wark scored as Bobby Robson took Town to Wembley by beating one of his former clubs.

Wembley's open spaces suited Ipswich's expansive style but until the closing stages when Osborne got the only goal of the final, Arsenal's goal led a charmed life. Three times the woodwork saved the Gunners, Wark twice hitting the post with the bar denying Mariner while Arsenal's legendary goalkeeper Pat Jennings made a brilliant save from a George Burley header.

David Geddis' direct running and tracking of marauding full back Sammy Nelson caused Arsenal problems all afternoon. Geddis' persistence paid off when his cross was only partially cleared into the path of Osborne who made no mistake but was so overcome with emotion he had to be withdrawn. A son of Suffolk, Osborne had been plucked from the Suffolk & Ipswich League in 1971 and his cup-winning goal was by far the highlight of his career.

BOBBY ROBSON

Bobby Robson's statue stands proudly outside Portman Road, joining that of Sir Alf Ramsey. Robson had won 20 caps for England and became manager of Ipswich in January 1969 - six years after Ramsey had left to take over at England. Robson would remain at Ipswich until 1982, combining the last four years of his reign with the role of England 'B' manager. Following in Ramsey's footsteps Robson left Ipswich only for his country. He managed England from 1982 to 1990, going closer than anyone to emulating Ramsey's achievement in guiding England to the World Cup, penalty shoot-out defeat in the semi final amidst Gazza's tears ended Robson's tenure.

England's near miss was reflected in Robson's era at Ipswich by runners' up positions in the top flight in 1981 and '82 but Robson was not a 'nearly man' - he led Ipswich to triumph in the FA Cup in 1978 and the UEFA Cup in 1981.

TEXACO CUP

The Texaco Cup rightly doesn't rank highly in the history of Ipswich Town, not when the League title, FA Cup and European glory are considered. However in winning the Texaco Cup in 1972-73 Ipswich did defeat Norwich City both home and away in the two-legged final so it holds its special place in Blues' memories.

The Texaco Cup began in 1970-71, intended as an international league Cup competition featuring teams from England, Scotland, Northern Ireland and the Republic of Ireland. Wolves were the first winners with Derby taking the trophy in 1972. Ipswich entered the competition in 1972-73 as Texaco began a separate tournament for Irish clubs leaving just English and Scottish clubs participating. Hearts and Airdrie had been runners' up in the first two years of the trophy but in 1972-73 the final was an all East Anglian affair, Ipswich triumphing 2-1 in each leg, 4-2 on aggregate.

Bobby Robson

CROWD PLEASER

ANSWERS ON PAGE 62

There are five famous Brits
hiding in the crowd...
can you find them?
#ITFC

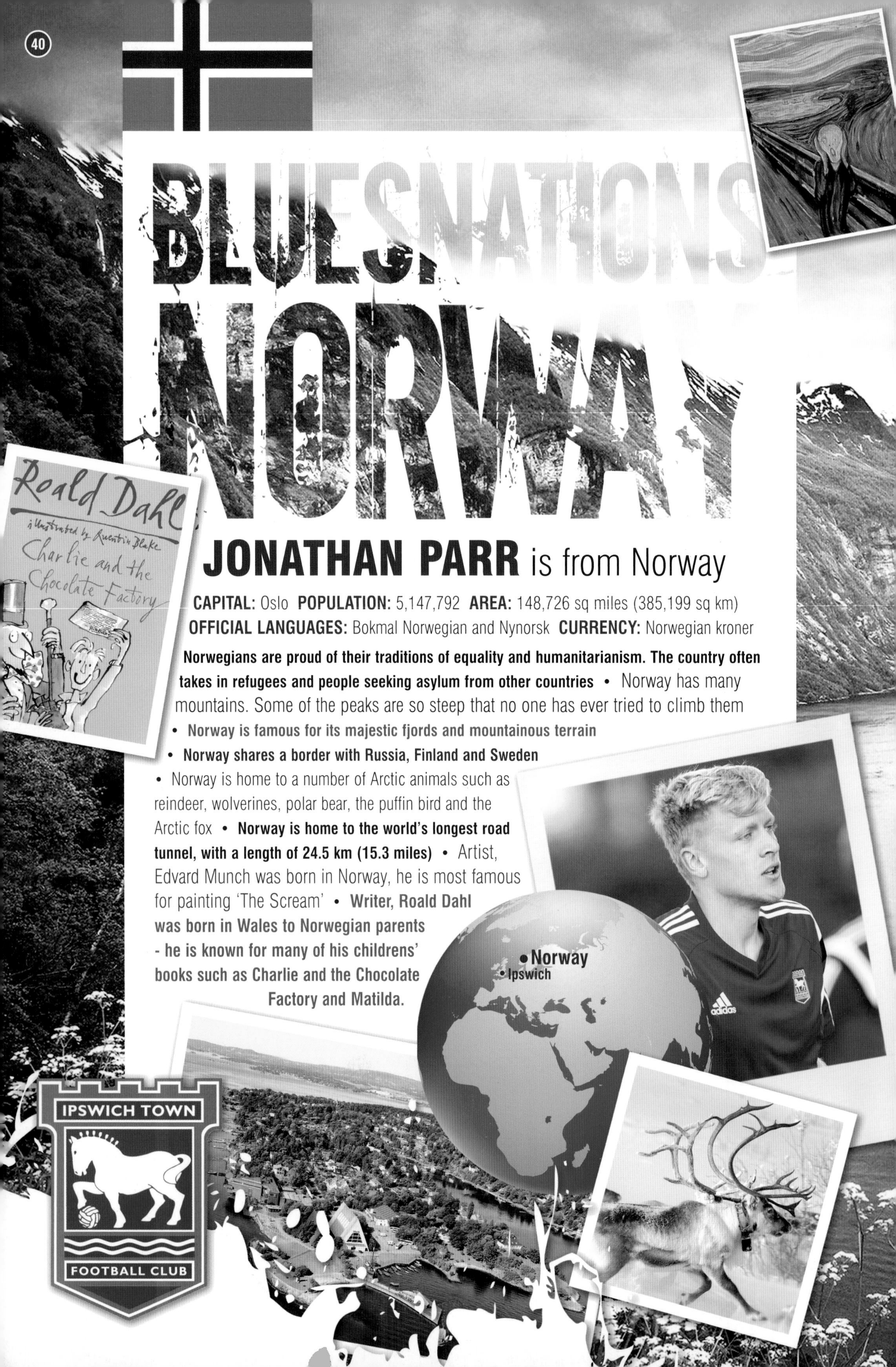

BLUESNATIONS NORWAY

JONATHAN PARR is from Norway

CAPITAL: Oslo **POPULATION:** 5,147,792 **AREA:** 148,726 sq miles (385,199 sq km) **OFFICIAL LANGUAGES:** Bokmal Norwegian and Nynorsk **CURRENCY:** Norwegian kroner

Norwegians are proud of their traditions of equality and humanitarianism. The country often takes in refugees and people seeking asylum from other countries • Norway has many mountains. Some of the peaks are so steep that no one has ever tried to climb them • **Norway is famous for its majestic fjords and mountainous terrain** • **Norway shares a border with Russia, Finland and Sweden** • Norway is home to a number of Arctic animals such as reindeer, wolverines, polar bear, the puffin bird and the Arctic fox • **Norway is home to the world's longest road tunnel, with a length of 24.5 km (15.3 miles)** • Artist, Edvard Munch was born in Norway, he is most famous for painting 'The Scream' • **Writer, Roald Dahl was born in Wales to Norwegian parents - he is known for many of his childrens' books such as Charlie and the Chocolate Factory and Matilda.**

CHRISTOPHE
BERRA
06
marcus evans

COLE SKUSE

FOOTIE FIRSTS

What were the first pair of boots you owned? Puma Kings

Who was the first big influence on your career and why? My Dad, he's been there since the start making big sacrifices

Which is your first goal that comes to mind? An overhead kick when I was young

BEST...

Best advice you've been given? Treat every day like it's your last

Best friend in football? Brian Wilson at Oldham

Best moment of my life? The birth of my daughter, Ava

IF I COULD...

Play any sportsman at their own game, it would be...? Lewis Hamilton, that would be a good race!

Have one superpower, it would be...? I would be 'Mr Hindsight' - hindsight is a wonderful thing!

Travel back in time, I would...? Go back to the seventies for the great music

FINALLY...

Something interesting you might not know about me is...? I got offered a scholarship to play basketball in America

TYRONE MINGS

FOOTIE FIRSTS

What were the first pair of boots you owned? Red Puma Kings

Who was the first big influence on your career and why? My Mum - she used to carry me on her back to and from training

Who was the first manager you played for - what was he like? A guy called Jamie Moss, he was very understanding - I was playing for the U6s!

BEST...

Best advice you've been given? Just work hard and have faith

Best sportsperson in the world? Jessica Ennis

Best moment of my life? Giving my sister away at her wedding

IF I COULD...

Have one superpower, it would be...? To rewind time

Re-live one moment in my career, it would be...? Making my debut at Burnley

Travel back in time, I would...? Put a big bet on me to play in the Championship when I was at Yate Town

FINALLY...

Something interesting you might not know about me is...? I can speak Spanish, French, German and Arabic!

STEPHEN HUNT

FOOTIE FIRSTS

What were the first pair of boots you owned? Puma Kings

When were you first spotted by a pro club?
I was 17 in a schools match

Which is your first goal that comes to mind?
For Brentford v Bournemouth

BEST...

Best advice you've been given? Never give up

Best friend in football? My brother, Noel Hunt

Best sportsperson in the world? Tiger Woods

IF I COULD...

Re-live one moment in my career, it would be...?
The goal that kept us up at Wolves!

Have one superpower, it would be...?
To heal the sick

Travel back in time, I would...?
Take golf lessons!

FINALLY...

Something interesting you might not know about me is...?
I own a Gastro Pub

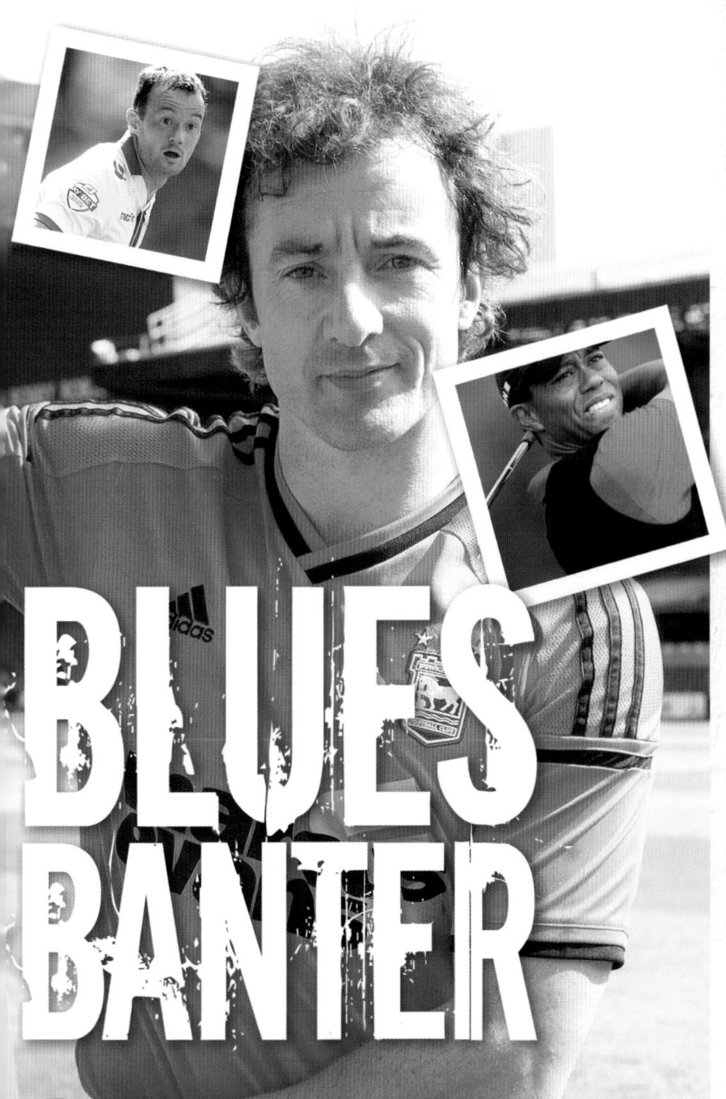

TOMMY SMITH

FOOTIE FIRSTS

What were the first pair of boots you owned?
A pair of black Adidas boots

Who was the first big influence on your career and why?
My Dad - he was my first coach

Which is your first goal that comes to mind?
Scoring from the halfway line for Crewe U9s

BEST...

Best advice you've been given?
A day of not giving your all is a day lost forever

Best team you've played against? Brazil in the Olympics

Best moment of my life?
Scoring the winner for New Zealand that put us through to the World Cup Play-Offs

IF I COULD...

Play any sportsman at their own game, it would be...? Rory McIlroy at golf

Travel back in time, I would...?
Buy shares of Apple when it first appeared!

Be best friends with anyone in the world, it would be...? David Beckham

FINALLY...

Something interesting you might not know about me is...?
I'm doing a degree in Sports Science

HUDDERSFIELD TOWN

GROUND: John Smith's Stadium
CAPACITY: 24,500 **MANAGER:** Chris Powell
NICKNAME: The Terriers

DID YOU KNOW: In 1926, Huddersfield became the first English team to win three successive league titles - no team has beaten this record!

LEEDS UNITED

GROUND: Elland Road **CAPACITY:** 39,460
MANAGER: TBC
NICKNAMES: The Whites, The Peacocks

DID YOU KNOW: Leeds United fans also have a salute which is known as the 'Leeds Salute'.

MIDDLESBROUGH

GROUND: Riverside Stadium
CAPACITY: 34,988 **HEAD COACH:** Aitor Karanka
NICKNAME: Boro

DID YOU KNOW: Middlesbrough won the League Cup in 2004, the club's first and only major trophy.

MILLWALL

GROUND: The Den **CAPACITY:** 20,146
MANAGER: Ian Holloway **NICKNAME:** The Lions

DID YOU KNOW: Millwall are ranked as 40th most successful club in English football - based on all results from their 86 seasons in the Football League from 1920-21 to 2013-14.

NORWICH CITY

GROUND: Carrow Road **CAPACITY:** 27,244
MANAGER: Neil Adams
NICKNAME: The Canaries

DID YOU KNOW: The fans' song "On the Ball, City" is regarded as being the oldest football song in the world.

NOTTINGHAM FOREST

GROUND: The City Ground **CAPACITY:** 30,576
MANAGER: Stuart Pearce
NICKNAMES: Forest, The Reds

DID YOU KNOW: Nottingham Forest's most successful period came under the management of Brian Clough, between 1975 and 1993.

READING

GROUND: Madejski Stadium
CAPACITY: 24,161 **MANAGER:** Nigel Adkins
NICKNAME: The Royals

DID YOU KNOW:
Established in 1871, Reading is one of the oldest teams in England.

ROTHERHAM

GROUND: New York Stadium **CAPACITY:** 12,021
MANAGER: Steve Evans **NICKNAME:** The Millers

DID YOU KNOW: After finishing 4th in League One last season, they won on penalties in the Play-Off final against Leyton Orient and were promoted to the Championship.

SHEFFIELD WEDNESDAY

GROUND: Hillsborough Stadium
CAPACITY: 39,732 **MANAGER:** Stuart Gray
NICKNAMES: The Owls, The Wednesday

DID YOU KNOW: Sheffield Wednesday were one of the founding members of The Premier League in 1992.

WATFORD

GROUND: Vicarage Road **CAPACITY:** 17,477
MANAGER: Oscar Garcia
NICKNAME: The Hornets

DID YOU KNOW: Sir Elton John serves alongside Graham Taylor as Watford's joint Honorary Life President.

WIGAN ATHLETIC

GROUND: DW Stadium **CAPACITY:** 25,138
MANAGER: Uwe Rösler **NICKNAME:** Latics

DID YOU KNOW: Wigan embarked on its first European campaign during the 2013-14 season in the UEFA Europa League group stages.

WOLVES

GROUND: Molineux **CAPACITY:** 30,852
MANAGER: Kenny Jackett
NICKNAME: Wolves

DID YOU KNOW:
Wolves have won the FA Cup four times - in 1893, 1908, 1949 and 1960!

DAVID McGOLDRICK 10

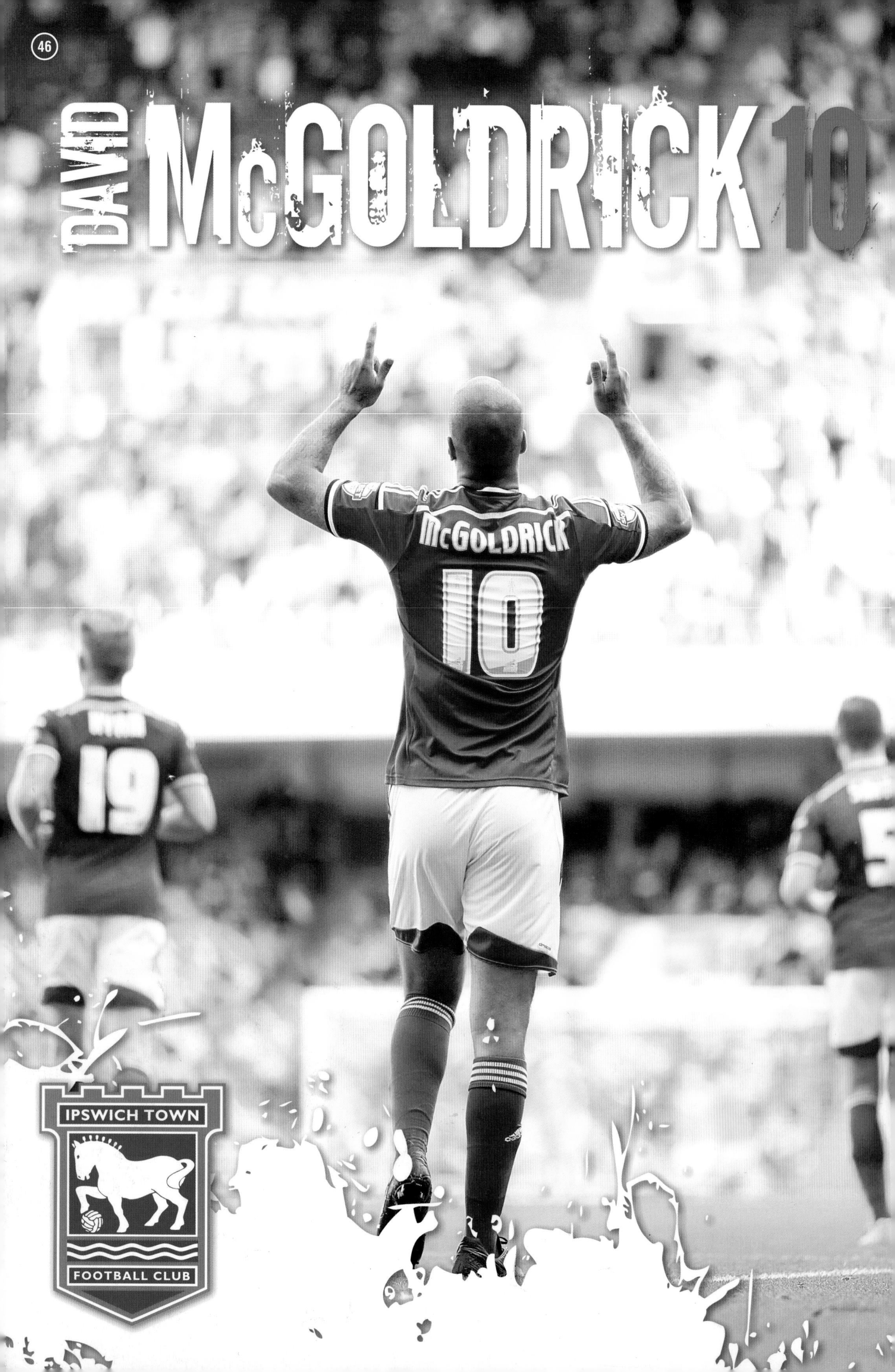
McGOLDRICK
10
19
IPSWICH TOWN
FOOTBALL CLUB

The search is on...

The surnames of Blues top scorers from the last 22 seasons are hidden in the grid, except for one... can you work out who?

```
T F M F A P T C T H O M S E N
S O A N R X N R O F R C P I O
G R U T P E K S A N V L E E N
D S K I O B H I M W Y B P V I
O T V E H U W P W J E D B M M
G E H S C O W C R O F T I A O
A R L B Z T U A N L M W S T H
N F L C E R C M O F D Y M H W
U M A S O N N P S G P J A I A
O Z H W A S T B N X D F T E L
C N S R G E X E H E S A B Q T
L J R K Y J K L O R L C E J E
B K A S M H Q L J F A U N T R
A Y M C G O L D R I C K T K S
I Q U K B I A A D Y T M S C P
```

Chris **Kiwomya**
Claus **Thomsen**
Alex **Mathie**
Ian **Marshall**
Paul **Mason**
James **Scowcroft**
David **Johnson**
Marcus **Bent**
Marcus **Stewart**
Pablo **Couñago**
Darren **Bent**
Shefki **Kuqi**
Nicky **Forster**
Alan **Lee**
Jonathan **Stead**
Jonathan **Walters**
David **Norris**
Michael **Chopra**
DJ **Campbell**
David **McGoldrick**

ANSWERS ON PAGE 62

DESIGN A STAR PLAYER

The transfer window opens in January. Who would you sign for Blues?

Imagine you wanted to sign a new central midfielder. Look at the qualities listed here and choose the main ones you'd like the Ipswich Town scouts out looking for.

List all of the qualities here in order with your most important quality as number one, the second most important thing as number two and so on. When you've done that estimate how much you'd be prepared to spend on the player you have identified.

You can also write the name of the player - already in the Championship or from elsewhere - that you think most fits the description you've come up with.

HEADING
He has to be able to head the ball like **TOMMY SMITH**

STAMINA
He has to have a 'good engine' like **LUKE HYAM**

SKILL
He has to have quick feet and tricks like **DAVID McGOLDRICK**

SHOOTING
He has to be able to shoot like **DARYL MURPHY**

VERSATILITY
He has to be able to play in more than one position like **LUKE CHAMBERS**

SHORT PASSING
He has to be able to keep possession like **COLE SKUSE**

CROSSING
He has to be able to cross the ball like **PAUL ANDERSON**

LONG PASSING
He has to be able to hit sweeping passes like **ELLIOTT HEWITT**

TACKLING
He has to be able to tackle like **CHRISTOPHE BERRA**

ATTITUDE
He has to have a good attitude like **JAY TABB**

	SKILL	PLAYER	PRICE
1			
2			
3			
4			
5			
6			
7			
8			
9			
10			

THE GOOD OLD DAYS 1980s

EIGHTIES EUROPEAN EXCITEMENT

The 1980s started with Ipswich in the top three of the top flight for three seasons running, be domestic cup semi finalists twice, quarter finalists once and win a European trophy! The rest of the decade wasn't as thrilling but the 80s were still a great time to watch football at Portman Road.

	Division	Position	
1979-80	Division 1	3rd of 22	FA Cup quarter finalists
1980-81	Division 1	2nd of 22	UEFA Cup winners FA Cup semi finalists
1981-82	Division 1	2nd of 22	League Cup semi finalists
1982-83	Division 1	9th of 22	
1983-84	Division 1	12th of 22	
1984-85	Division 1	17th of 22	League Cup semi finalists FA Cup quarter finalists
1985-86	Division 1	20th of 22	
1986-87	Division 2	5th of 22	Play off semi finalists
1987-88	Division 2	8th of 22	
1988-89	Division 2	8th of 22	

Arnold Muhren & Frans Thijssen

1981 UEFA CUP FINAL, SECOND LEG. AZ ALKMAAR V IPSWICH TOWN, OLYMPIC STADIUM, AMSTERDAM. FRANS THIJSSEN IS CONGRATULATED BY HIS TEAM MATES AFTER SCORING THE FIRST GOAL

MICK MILLS

UEFA CUP WINNERS

Bobby Robson went on to manage successfully across Europe and in 1980-81 he didn't just put Ipswich Town's name on a major European trophy - he did in in style. Ipswich won the UEFA Cup (Now the Europa League) by playing attractive passing football.

John Wark took a liking to the competition, scoring 14 goals in all including the decisive one in the final. He began with four in Town's first game as Aris Salonika were beaten 5-1. Three of his goals were penalties with the Greek side's also coming from the spot. Salonika won the second leg 3-1 but Blues went through comfortably.

Wark was at it again in the second round, scoring twice in a 3-0 first leg win over Bohemians of Prague and while the return leg was lost 2-0, again the home leg had seen Town build what proved to be a big enough lead.

The second leg of the third round game against Widzew Lodz in Poland was lost 1-0 but that score-line didn't put much of a dent in the 5-0 lead established in the first leg, Wark again claiming a hat-trick.

The quarter-final saw Town travel for the first leg. Undaunted, they once again established a big first leg lead, winning 4-1 in France against St. Etienne. The French outfit had been as free-scoring as Ipswich. When 1978 Dutch World Cup star Johnny Rep opened the scoring it gave them an aggregate of 23-0 in the competition! However Wark again got on the score-sheet as Ipswich ran riot and a penalty saw him do so again in the home leg where a 3-1 win produced a convincing 7-2 aggregate. Ipswich would win both legs of the semi final too, but 1-0 in each leg illustrated tight games with Cologne. Inevitably Wark scored the winner in the first leg at home while Terry Butcher came up smelling of roses in the second leg in Germany.

While Wark's goals grabbed him the headlines, much of Ipswich's stylish soccer stemmed from the 'Double-Dutch' combination of midfielders Arnold Muhren and Frans Thijssen whose slick movement and passing did so much to make Ipswich the team they were. Thijssen would join Wark in scoring in both legs of the final against AZ 67 Alkmaar of Holland. Their goals were needed in the second leg in Holland, Thijssen's goal there being a 20 yard volley after four minutes that left the new Dutch champions needing to score five. Paul Mariner's sixth goal of the competition in the 3-0 first leg victory helped to steer Blues home but it was a close run thing as AZ scored four in front of their own fans.

Having reduced the aggregate score to 2-4 they saw that man Wark restore a three goal cushion which proved just enough as AZ scored two more to record an aggregate of 4-5. Ipswich were the UEFA Cup winners!

BEST TEAM IN THE COUNTRY?

No-one should ever consider winning a major European trophy to be a disappointment but in 1980-81 Ipswich could claim to be the best team in the country. They could so easily have won the league title and maybe the FA Cup as well. A fixture pile up eventually cost Town the title. League leaders for most of the season, they won only two of the last eight games.

Ironically one of those was away to Aston Villa who eventually pipped Town to the title. Ipswich had knocked Villa out of the FA Cup in the third round allowing them to focus on the league. Ipswich reached the semi final of the FA Cup, going down 2-1 to Manchester City.

EUROPEAN FOOTBALL

Ipswich first played European football when entering the European Cup in 1961-62 and most recently played in Europe in 2002-03 and 2001-02. The golden age of Town's involvement in Europe stretches from 1982-83 back to 1973-74 when Real Madrid were beaten. During that spell Ipswich appeared in Europe for nine seasons out of 10. Town's last European game of the eighties was a 3-1 home win over Roma in 1982-83, a memorable night but not quite sufficient to overturn a 3-0 first leg score-line.

John Wark

Can you work out the odd one out in each grid?

ANSWERS ON PAGE 62

ODD ONE OUT

The Writing's on the Wall...

Decorate this wall and show your love for Ipswich...

PAUL ANDERSON 11

BADGE OF HONOUR

Since 1972 Ipswich Town's badge has been relatively simple and dominated by a Suffolk Punch horse.

Previously the club's badge had been based on the coat of arms of the Borough Council. Part of this badge included a ship with three masts that formed part of the town's seal since the 13th century. Other emblems included sea-horses to indicate Ipswich's connection with the sea while a golden lion representing England was also often prominent.

The modern club bade was the work of a former treasurer of the supporters club, John Gammage. He came up with the winning design in a competition for a new badge. Mr. Gammage felt that the Punch horse was a highly respected sporting horse and based his design around that as an emblem, with a football under one of its feet.

Ipswich's connection with the sea is included in the modern badge by the wavy lines at the bottom with the town's historic buildings paid tribute to by the turreting which since the mid nineties has been at the top of the badge.

AROUND THE CHAMPIONSHIP: There are a mixture of traditional and modern badges in the rest of the Championship and here we look at a selection of them.

BIRMINGHAM CITY:

Like Ipswich's, Birmingham City's current badge came from a competition. In their case it came from a local newspaper competition.

Birmingham's badge began life in 1972, just a decade after the club excelled in the early years of European competition. The idea of a globe above a football was to indicate the club's international ambitions.

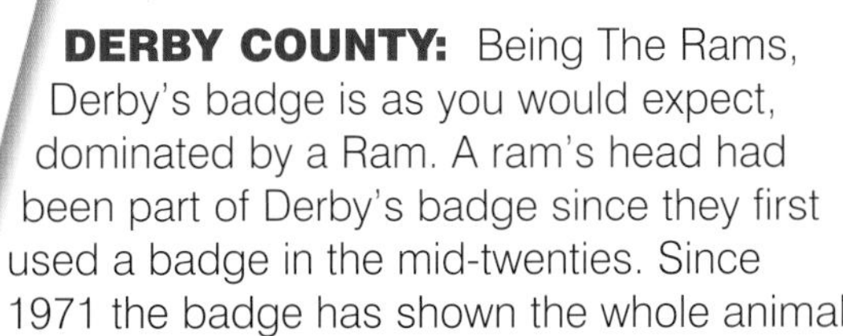

DERBY COUNTY: Being The Rams, Derby's badge is as you would expect, dominated by a Ram. A ram's head had been part of Derby's badge since they first used a badge in the mid-twenties. Since 1971 the badge has shown the whole animal.

MIDDLESBROUGH:

Middlesbrough's modern badge went back to the beginning by replacing the date 1986 with 1876. This was to re-introduce the date of the club's original formation rather than the date it was reformed following a financial disaster that saw it go into liquidation in 1986. The badge shows a red lion in a shield headed by the name of the town with the words Football Club joining the date at the foot of the emblem.

WOLVERHAMPTON WANDERERS:

Obviously a wolf was inevitably going to become the dominant object on this badge! It started to prowl in the 1970s and for a while there were three wolves on Wolves' badge but since the early 1980s it has been the head of a single wolf on the club's badge.

NOTTINGHAM FOREST: Like a lot of clubs, Forest's initial badge was based on the coat of arms of their city. The modern day Forest badge is the work of graphic artist David Lewis who came up with the badge in 1973. It signalled a new start and came at the right time as Forest soon entered the most glorious part of their history. The wavy lines on their badge indicate the River Trent, rather than being near to the sea as on Ipswich's badge. The tree that makes up most of the badge indicates the famous Sherwood Forest.

SHEFFIELD WEDNESDAY:

Animals often become emblems with which clubs become associated. In the case of Sheffield Wednesday their owl comes from the fact that the club has long been based in the suburb of Owlerton, although a century ago Owlerton was incorporated into Hillsborough which of course is now the name of The Owls' home ground.

Nowadays the badge has a simple drawing of an owl within a shield, together with the year of foundation, 1867 showing the Owls' wisdom comes from being one of the oldest clubs in the country.

COLE
SKUSE
08
marcus evans
adidas

Can you match each of these faces to the Ipswich Town player they belong to?

DAVID McGOLDRICK · PAUL ANDERSON · PAUL TAYLOR · ANTHONY WORDSWORTH

CHRISTOPHE BERRA · BARTOSZ BIALKOWSKI · TYRONE MINGS · LUKE HYAM · FRANK NOUBLE

ANSWERS ON PAGE 62

CHAMPIONSHIP Predictions

Here are our predictions for 2015... See if you agree?

WINNERS: IPSWICH TOWN

YOUR PREDICTION:

22ND: BRENTFORD

YOUR PREDICTION:

RUNNERS UP: EVERTON

YOUR PREDICTION:

RUNNERS UP: FULHAM

YOUR PREDICTION:

RELEGATION

23RD: ROTHERHAM

YOUR PREDICTION:

FA CUP

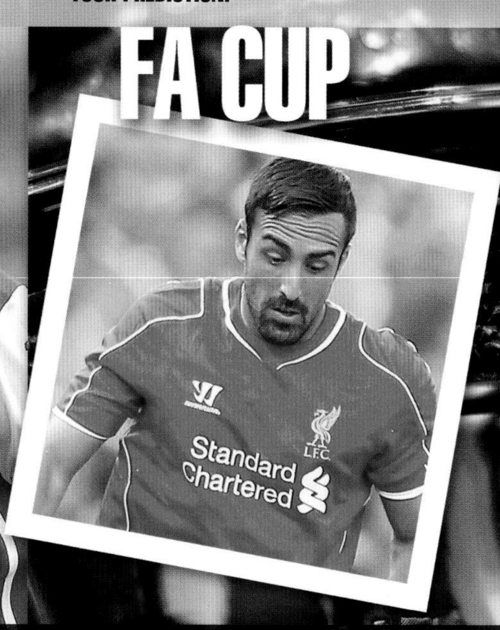

WINNERS: LIVERPOOL

YOUR PREDICTION:

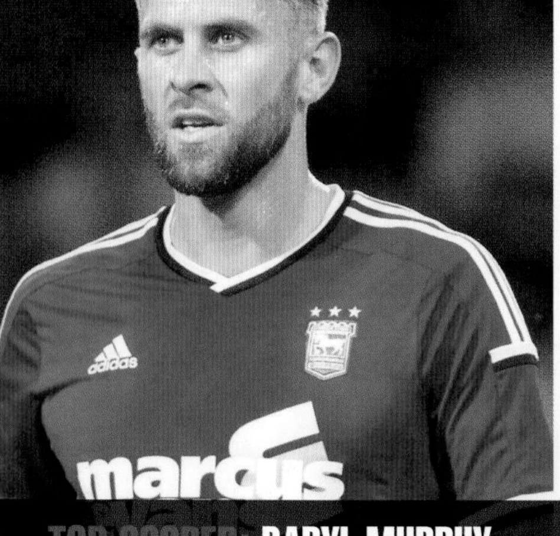

TOP SCORER: DARYL MURPHY

YOUR PREDICTION:

24TH: NORWICH CITY

YOUR PREDICTION:

TOP SCORER: DANIEL STURRIDGE

YOUR PREDICTION:

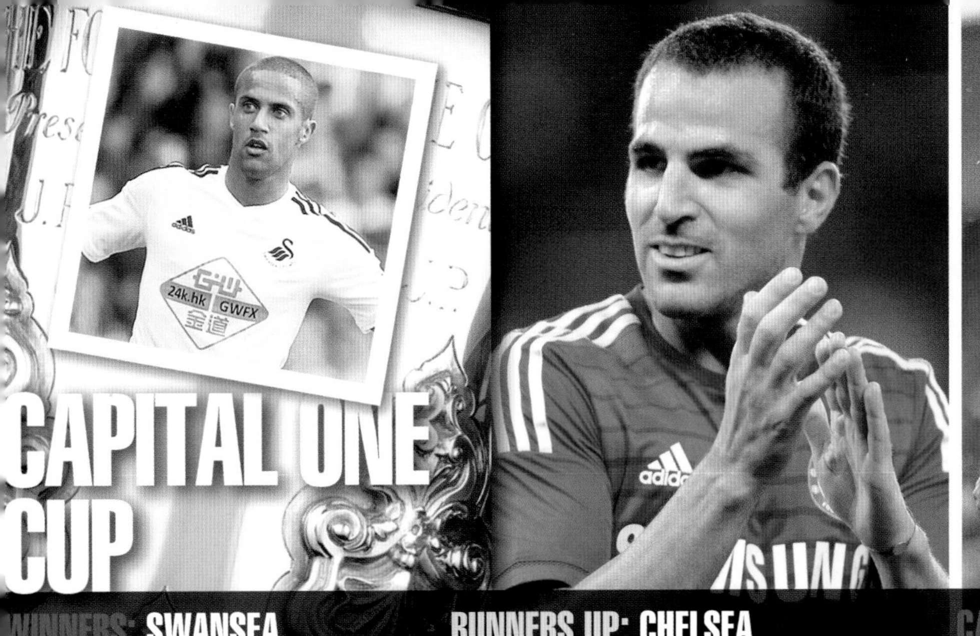

CAPITAL ONE CUP

FIRST IPSWICH PLAYER TO FIND THE NET IN 2015

WINNERS: SWANSEA

YOUR PREDICTION:

RUNNERS UP: CHELSEA

YOUR PREDICTION:

CAMERON STEWART

YOUR PREDICTION:

PREMIER LEAGUE

2015

DERBY DAY SCORE FEBRUARY 2015

RUNNERS UP: MAN CITY

YOUR PREDICTION:

WINNERS: MAN UTD

YOUR PREDICTION:

NORWICH 1 IPSWICH 3

YOUR PREDICTION:

TOP SCORER: WILFRIED BONY

YOUR PREDICTION:

TOP SCORER: WAYNE ROONEY

YOUR PREDICTION:

PAGE 9 · THE BIG MATCH

A. Ray Crawford - 204, B. Alan Brazil - 70, C. Michael Chopra - 18, D. Paul Mariner - 96, E. Eric Gates - 73, F. Jay Emmanuel-Thomas - 8, G. Arnold Muhren - 21, H. Jason Dozzell - 54, I. Mick Mills - 22

PAGE 26 · THE BIG MATCH

A. Wigan Athletic, B. Watford, C. Norwich City, D. Charlton Athletic, E. Brighton & Hove Albion, F. Derby County, G. Nottingham Forest, H. Fulham, I. Wolverhampton Wanderers

PAGE 32 · GUESS WHO

1. Cameron Stewart, 2. Christophe Berra, 3. Frederic Veseli, 4. Teddy Bishop, 5. Luke Chambers, 6. Cole Skuse, 7. Michael Crowe, 8. Daryl Murphy

PAGE 35 · THE BIG MATCH

A. Roger Osborne - 124, B. Alan Hunter - 280, C. John Wark - 509, D. Carlos Edwards - 166, E. George Burley - 394, F. Kevin Beattie - 228, G. Frans Thijssen - 125, H. Terry Butcher - 271, I. Matt Holland - 258

PAGE 38 · CROWD PLEASER

David Tennant, Kate Middleton, Nick Grimshaw, Holly Willoughby and Hugh Grant

PAGE 47 · THE SEARCH IS ON...

David Norris

PAGE 53 · ODD ONE OUT

1. B - John Terry did not appear in the England 2014 FIFA World Cup squad.
2. D - Philipp Lahm is German, the other players are Spanish.
3. C - Helen Flanagan is not married to a footballer.
4. A - Eric Djemba Djemba is from Cameroon, the other players are from Ghana.
5. C - Murphy is a striker, the other players are defenders.
6. B - Samuel Eto'o plays for Everton, the other images relate to Birmingham City.
7. A - Jay Tabb does not relate to New Zealand.
8. D - Brian Clough did not mange Ipswich Town.
9. A - The Wear Bridge is in Sunderland, the other images represent Middlesbrough.
10. A - Elliott Hewitt is Welsh, the other players are English.

PAGE 59 · THE BIG MATCH

A. Bartosz Bialkowski, B. Paul Taylor, C. Luke Hyam, D. Paul Anderson, E. Anthony Wordsworth, F. Frank Nouble, G. Tyrone Mings, H. David McGoldrick, I. Christophe Berra